MW01178160

To

from

Santa Lives!

The Night Before Christmas

DIANNE MORITZ

Illustrated by Jackie Pardo

 Peter Pauper Press, Inc.
White Plains, New York

For Judy Byerly and my mother

Designed by Heather Zschock

Illustrations copyright © 2004 Jackie Pardo
www.artscounselinc.com

Copyright © 2004
Peter Pauper Press, Inc.
202 Mamaroneck Avenue
White Plains, NY 10601
ISBN 0-88088-467-3
Printed in China
7 6 5 4 3 2 1

Visit us at www.peterpauper.com

Santa Lives!

The Night Before Christmas

Think of that cute but cynical girl in "Miracle on 34th Street." That was me. I don't remember ever believing in Santa Claus. Years later, when I was teaching first grade, a little boy announced, "Santa's not real, is he Ms. Moritz?"

As I looked out into thirty two sweet, innocent faces, I knew in

a moment the need for all things
mysterious and mythical.

"Yes, Santa is real."

'Tis the night before Christmas

and time for
amends

to all little
children and
long-ago friends.

You see,
as a tyke,

I called Santa
a fake,

smashed illusions of pals,

and caused
them
heartache.

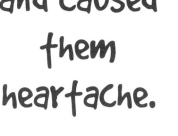

"oh, Judy," I said,
"there is no St. Nick!

"And if you
believe,

you're a
dummy, not
quick!"

Judy's mom got so mad, she yelled at my mother,

who right then
declared me

a neighborhood bother.

It's true that
with age

I have gained some insight.

It's time for me now

to set old
wrongs to
right.

Yes, Judy, Virginia,
there is
Santa Claus.

(Just wait
all you
Scrooges—

please hold

your

"pshaws.")

The old
Christmas
wonder

and magic
we
weave,

have rekindled faith

on this new
christmas
eve.

Believing in Santa

is not
infantile,

for Santa
exists

in a gift . . .
in a smile.

Yes, Santa's alive
in those
red-suited elves,

And Santa claus lives

in our
hearts . . .
in ourselves.

Santa lives on in our thoughts

and our prayers,

and Santa is
simply

someone who cares.

a jolly old elf

who brings
love and toys.

forgive me,
dear Judy,
I must eat
humble pie.

our long-ago spat

has helped open my eyes.

Now the stockings are hung;

Lights are
aglow;

The Children are sleeping;

It's beginning to snow.

So, mothers
and dads,

for past sins
I'm contrite.

Now I'm off to bake cookies— Santa's coming tonight!

Merry Christmas to All, and to All a Good-Night!

And a Happy New Year!